In My ~~Place~~

The Spirituality of Substitution

Gary Jenkins

Vicar of St Peter's Church, St Helier, Morden

GROVE BOOKS LIMITED
RIDLEY HALL RD CAMBRIDGE CB3 9HU

Contents

Dedicated, in his retirement year, to Peter Ronayne who for many years has proclaimed faithfully the message of Christ crucified to the people of inner London.

Acknowledgements
I would like to acknowledge the help of Martin Davie, Mark Knight, Jason Lavender, Leslie Wells, and the library of Oak Hill College in the preparation of this booklet.

The Cover Illustration is by Peter Ashton

First Impression November 1999
ISSN 0262-799X
ISBN 1 85174 418 5

1
The Power of Substitution

In my place condemned he stood;
sealed my pardon with his blood:
Alleluia! what a saviour.[1]

Few doctrines have been so consistently unpopular among theologians as the doctrine of substitutionary atonement. It has been variously described as immoral, unjust, incomprehensible, unchristian, incredible and outdated. Few doctrines, however, have brought so much joy, assurance, comfort and hope to the Christian believer. Charles Spurgeon, the great nineteenth-century Baptist preacher to the teeming hordes of London, maintained:

> If there should ever come a wretched day when all the pulpits shall be full of modern thought, and the old doctrine of substitutionary sacrifice shall be exploded, there will remain no word of comfort for the guilty or hope for the despairing. Hushed will be for ever those silken notes which console the living and cheer the dying.[2]

The doctrine of substitution continues to lie at the heart of evangelical spirituality today. David Gillett writes of the substitutionary death of Christ on the cross:

> Nothing else in earth or heaven is as vital to evangelicals as the objective truth of the cross and a person's conscious acceptance of all that it offers as God's gracious provision of forgiveness, reconciliation, and eternal life.[3]

This doctrine is preached from the pulpits of many growing churches. It is the subject of scores of popular hymns and choruses. It has been proclaimed by some of our greatest evangelists from D L Moody to Billy Graham. It features in some of the most widely known evangelistic resources from *Alpha* to *Emmaus*. It was loved by the Reformers of the sixteenth century and was at the heart of the revival of the eighteenth. The *Book of Common Prayer,* the Articles of the Church of England,[4] and other Reformation formularies bear witness to it.

---

1   Bliss, P, *Hymns for Today's Church* (Hodder & Stoughton, 1982) No 130.
2   Gillett, D K, *Trust and Obey: Explorations in Evangelical Spirituality* (London: Darton, Longman & Todd, 1993) p 7.
3   Gillett, *op cit,* p 67.
4   See 'Appendix: Salvation and the Anglican Heritage' in Doctrine Commission of the General Synod of the Church of England, *The Mystery of Salvation* (London: Church House Publishing, 1995) pp 206–216.

Far from being unbelievable and incomprehensible, the doctrine of substitution is held to by many people who claim to have had their lives changed by it. This old doctrine that stubbornly refuses to die, this 'irrelevant' relic from the past, annoyingly persists in demonstrating its power to change lives. Even its critics admit it 'preaches well.' Defending it, Gillett explains why:

> An exposition of substitutionary atonement allows the whole mystery of the cross to be communicated in manageable compass: the hearer is given a step by step explanation of the relationship between the eternal God, the historical event of Calvary, and his or her present spiritual state. The need for a response can be clearly shown and the way opened for the individual to enter here and now into the benefits of what Christ did two thousand years ago.[5]

I wish to argue the particular relevance of the substitutionary atonement to the people who live in urban priority areas and outer housing estates, of the kind that I am privileged to live amongst and serve. Of course, substitution is relevant to all, but I believe the message of 'Christ in my place' is *especially* good news in this cultural setting. Why? Because it addresses directly and personally two of the chief problems people wrestle with in a way that no other understanding of the atonement does. These two problems are feelings of guilt and of low self-worth.

I hope to show how substitution speaks directly to these and, in the process of doing so, to argue for the importance of regaining and maintaining a living contemporary spirituality centred on substitutionary atonement.

---

5   Gillett, *op cit*, p 73.

2
Why Substitution?

Amazing love, O what sacrifice,
The Son of God given for me.
My debt He pays, and my death He dies,
That I might live, that I might live.[6]

Substitution in Scripture

The first and most obvious answer to the question 'why substitution' is that this is how God decided to do it. From early on in Scripture the principle of substitution[7] can be discerned. It comes to its fullest expression at the cross[8] where Jesus took the place of, or substituted himself, for sinners.

The Bible does not explain *why* God chose to operate in this way; but that he did so seems to be in harmony with his general mode of operation as revealed in Scripture.

Substitution is, of course, closely related to incarnation, though sometimes those who most stress the incarnation as a principle for Christian living and ministry are least happy with the idea of substitution. However, on the basis of scriptural revelation it would be wrong to set the two in opposition for two main reasons.

Firstly, incarnation led to substitution. It was the *incarnate* Lord who substituted himself for sinners on the cross. Jesus was the man born to die. When he took flesh and became a human being he did so in order to save humankind through his death and resurrection, which included him dying as a substitute and taking our place. He was a suitable substitute for us because he was one of us—he was fully human—as well as fully God. Rembrandt's famous painting of the nativity which shows the shadow of the cross in the background nicely makes the connection between incarnation and atonement.

Secondly, substitution is the incarnation taken to its logical conclusion. If the incarnation is about the Son of God coming to live in our world, sharing and identifying with our joys and our sorrows and our lives to the extent of taking flesh and dwelling amongst us, then substitutionary atonement speaks of that same Jesus coming to us in our sadness and guilt and even in our judgment

---

6 Kendrick, G, 'My Lord what love is this?' in *Songs of Fellowship* (Eastbourne: Kingsway Music, 1998) No 398.

7 The provision of the ram which dies instead of Isaac in Genesis 22 is clearly substitutionary in character as is the passover lamb of Exodus 12. Later on in the Old Testament Isaiah 53 is, of course, a key text.

8 The principal New Testament texts are Mark 10.45, Galatians 3.13, Romans 3.21-26, 1 Corinthians 5.7, Hebrews 9.28, 1 Peter 1.19, 1 Peter 2.24, 1 Timothy 2.6, John 11.50, 2 Corinthians 5.14, 2 Corinthians 5.21.

before God and standing there in our place, for us and instead of us. Substitution is, therefore, a working out of the incarnational principle:

> ...on the cross Jesus' representative relation to us, as the last Adam whose image we are to bear, took the form of substituting for us under judgment, as the suffering servant on whom the Lord 'laid the iniquity of us all.'[9]

Substitution is also a strongly Trinitarian doctrine that can only be properly understood in Trinitarian terms. Some of its fiercest critics have failed to take this into account, and to be fair, so have some of its chief proponents, whose clumsy presentations of the doctrine have brought it into disrepute. Unsatisfactory representations of substitution characteristically divide the persons of the Trinity, often pitting them against each other. Various stories and analogies used over the years to convey the truth of substitution fall into this trap.

One example is Nicky Gumbel's illustration in his otherwise admirable exposition of the cross in the *Alpha* source book *Questions of Life*[10] in which an innocent prisoner of war substitutes himself for the sake of his comrades and dies at the hands of a sadistic Japanese guard. Apart from the moral problems involved in equating this evil guard with a loving God, the illustration suffers from the fatal flaw of having three parties: the guard (who presumably represents God), the POW (who represents Jesus) and the saved men. Gumbel offers this as an illustration of the self-substitution of God but it is precisely *not* that, since it is not the guard but a third party who substitutes himself. This perhaps shows, if nothing else, the difficulty of finding illustrations that do justice to substitution.

An effective explanation of substitution, in contrast, must reckon with the essential unity of the persons of the Trinity, working together in the great act of salvation:

> Any notion of penal substitution in which three independent actors play a part—the guilty party, the punitive judge, and the innocent victim—is to be repudiated with the utmost vehemence, for Christ is not an independent third person but the eternal Son of the Father, who is one with the Father in his essential being.[11]

There are only two parties involved in the atonement: the believer and the Lord. We are dealing with the self-substitution of God and not with God sending someone else, quite separate from himself, to take the blame on behalf of sinful humanity.[12] It is God, in the person of his Son, who stands in the place of sinners.

9 Packer, J I, 'What Did the Cross Achieve? The Logic of Penal Substitution,' in *Tyndale Bulletin*, 25, 1974, p 34.
10 Gumbel, N, *Questions of Life* (Eastbourne: Kingsway, 1993) p 47.
11 Stott, J R W, *The Cross of Christ* (Leicester: Inter-Varsity Press, 1986) p 158.
12 Stott, *op cit*, pp 133-163.

But why should this be the manner of God's saving purposes? Ultimately we cannot know. This must remain a mystery and indeed there are deep mysteries involved in contemplating the work of God in atonement. The cross is challenging to human wisdom and surprising to human expectation. To those who look for power, it appears weak. To those who look for wisdom, it seems foolishness. But, to those with eyes to see, it is the power of God and the wisdom of God.[13] God in his wisdom chose to do it this way and in this way his full power and wisdom is seen and displayed.

John Stott argues that substitution is more than a theory of the atonement, being in fact the 'heart of the atonement' and the essence of the various biblical images used to describe it.[14] Others have argued that the fact of substitution is simply inescapable. Colin Gunton states:

> At issue is the actuality of the atonement: whether the real evil of the world is faced and healed *ontologically* in the life, death, and resurrection of Jesus. To put it another way, we have to say that Jesus is our substitute because he does what we cannot do for ourselves. That includes undergoing the judgment of God, because were we to undergo it without him it would mean our destruction. Therefore the 'for us' of the cross and resurrection must *include*, though it is not exhausted by an 'instead of.'[15]

Penal Substitution?
Not all advocates of substitution have been prepared to speak in terms of *penal* substitution. Theologians such as Tom Smail have wanted to say 'substitution, yes; *penal* substitution, no.'[16] The essential question here is whether Christ in his death bore the *punishment* for sin. This is a complex argument and there is not the space to explore it in detail here, but, along with most of the authors I quote, I operate in this study with an understanding of substitution that includes a penal dimension. This has most impact in chapter three where I deal with substitution and guilt. At this point the penal aspect of substitution speaks most powerfully.

The Personal Impact of Substitution
If the first reason why substitution is important is that the Bible teaches it, the second is the pastoral power of substitution in people's lives. Although this by no means exhausts the achievement or the significance of the cross, I will argue

---

13 1 Corinthians 1.18–25.
14 Stott, *op cit*, p 203.
15 Gunton, C E, *The Actuality of the Atonement* (T & T Clark, 1988) p 165.
16 See for example his contribution in the St John's College, Nottingham symposium: Goldingay, J (ed), *Atonement Today* (London: SPCK, 1995) p 145 and his book *Once and for All: A Confession of the Cross* (London: Darton, Longman & Todd, 1998). Penal substitution is defended in books and articles by George Carey, John Stott and James Packer, referred to elsewhere in this study and also by Christina Baxter in the St John's symposium.

that substitution speaks particularly and powerfully to those who feel a profound sense of guilt and to those who feel a deep sense of worthlessness and lack
of personal significance.

As my witnesses I shall call some members of my church in our large council
estate parish in southwest London and also some of the writers of popular Christian worship songs. Happily, singing about the cross is undergoing something of
a renaissance.[17] These songs are indicators of the current state of spirituality in
the churches which are growing and where most younger people worship.

The great strength of a substitutionary understanding of the atonement is
that it presents the cross as an objective event—something definite that actually
happened, something decisive that occurred *then* which affects things *now*. Objective theories of atonement stand in contrast to subjective models such as that
generally attributed to Abelard, where the chief effect of the cross is seen in the
subject—in the change that is wrought in the life of the believer in his or her
contemplation of the cross and the following of it by way of example and not in
any objective change in the external world. There are, of course, other models of
the atonement that present the cross as an objective event; for example, the *Christus
Victor*[18] model which, as the name implies, stresses the objective victory of Christ
over the devil and the powers of evil. But the particular strength of substitution
is the way it links the objective historical event of the cross with the life of the
believer here and now.

With substitution, the cross is an event that affects me personally, here and
now. It is not merely a historical event consigned to the past. Nor does it just
affect me in the sense that what it achieved has some effect on me now—in much
the same way as the victory of the Second World War affects me now as a citizen
of the UK in 1999 who enjoys the benefit of not living under Nazi tyranny.[19]
Instead, the cross affects me personally because it was *my* death Jesus died, it
was *my* sin he bore, it was *my* judgment he underwent. And because of all this, I
can say with the apostle Paul 'the son of God loved *me* and gave himself for *me*'
or in the words of a contemporary worship song, 'Thank you Jesus, for loving
me.'[20]

Of course, a possible criticism of this approach is that it is too individualistic.
Some argue that a spirituality of substitution leads to an undue emphasis on the
life and experience of the individual at the expense of the more collective and

---

17 See especially songs by Graham Kendrick or Matt Redman in collections such as *Songs of
Fellowship* (Eastbourne: Kingsway Music, 1998).

18 Aulen, G, *Christus Victor* (London: SPCK, 1961).

19 This would be the kind of way that the *Christus Victor* model of the atonement could be said to
affect individuals. It affects them because they share in the benefits of the victory achieved and
not in the sense (as it would be with substitution) that they are personally involved in the
event of the cross themselves. In advocating substitution, the insights of the *Christus Victor*
model are not denied since it, too, witnesses to an important strand of New Testament
teaching about the cross.

20 *Songs of Fellowship*, No 523.

corporate aspects of the Christian faith. This is problematic in Western societies which are already excessively individualistic. It must be conceded at once that modern evangelical and charismatic Christianity *is* often overly individualistic but it is not of the essence of substitution that it is understood in these terms. For example, most of the New Testament letters which speak of substitution are addressed not to individuals (as we often read them) but to churches; thus the context in which the substitutionary atonement is presented is not itself an individualistic one.

In this booklet I have been careful to use the term 'personal' and not 'individual' because there is an important distinction between the two terms. 'Individual' has the sense of meaning 'single, particular, designed for one person' whereas 'person' has the sense of 'existing as a person, not an abstraction or a thing.' Substitution, though it affects individuals, is not an *individualistic* theory of the atonement but a *personal* one. At the heart of substitution there is a *personal* link between the crucified Lord and the believer. This is the language of relationships and substitution is thus the most relational understanding of the atonement.

To dismiss substitution, as some of its critics do, as no more than a legal fiction or an impersonal and incredible mechanism for the transferring of sin, or what Edward Irving called 'stock-exchange divinity' is fundamentally to misunderstand it.[21] Properly understood, substitution is about how the Trinitarian God, the God who has relationships at his heart, relates to the sinner personally and relationally through the cross.

There is nothing impersonal about substitution. Only a substitutionary understanding of the atonement gives that direct, personal, here-and-now connection between Jesus who died on the cross around AD 30 and the modern day believer. The cross is no longer a remote event from the distant past but something that affects me personally *now*. As to how it affects the individual believer we now turn.

---

21 Letham, R, *The Work of Christ* (Leicester: Inter-Varsity Press, 1993) p 138. Letham describes how penal substitution can seem a 'heartless business transaction' when detached from the Bible's wider frame of reference.

3

Substitution and Guilt

No condemnation now I dread
Jesus and all in him, is mine!
Alive in him, my living head,
and clothed in righteousness divine,
Bold I approach the eternal throne
And claim the crown, through Christ my own.[22]

Are we less worried about our sins than were a previous generation about theirs? If so, are we even less worried about a negative divine reaction to them? Are we, as Tom Smail has argued, more likely to see ourselves as *victims* than *villains?*[23] Are we more concerned with our suffering than our sin?

Almost certainly the answer to each of these questions is 'yes.' If we think about God at all today we are far more likely to ask 'How can God allow so much suffering in the world?' rather than 'What must I do to be saved?' This has produced a change in the focus of teaching about the cross in much modern theological thinking from atonement to theodicy. The cross is presented less as the answer to our sin and much more, by way of God's identification with a suffering world, as the answer to our pain.

This raises an important question. If we are much less concerned about the problem of sin, are we, therefore, much less interested and receptive to the traditional message of forgiveness won by Christ's death on the cross? If we no longer ask the 'sin-question,' are we still interested in the 'sin-answer'?

Whilst it is undoubtedly true that in our culture there is much less sense of being guilty *before* God and very little apparent awareness of the need to be right with him, in many people there remains a deep awareness of guilt in their lives. It may not be understood primarily in a Godward sense, which is surely a result of a secular society where God is pushed to the margins and very little is seen in terms of God and his will and purposes.

Today there may be far less a sense of objective moral guilt before the Creator, and many more largely unfocussed guilt *feelings*, but it remains common in pastoral ministry to encounter individuals who carry a deep burden of guilt often connected with the past. Sometimes, of course, this is *false guilt*. The person is not morally guilty in any real sense at all, but is, for whatever reason, troubled by deep *feelings* of guilt. Such people need not so much forgiveness as help to come

---

22 Wesley, C, *Hymns for Today's Church* (London: Hodder & Stoughton, 1982) No 588.
23 See chapter 3 'One Cross—Theodicy or Atonement?' in Smail, T, *Once and for All: A Confession of the Cross* (London: Darton, Longman & Todd, 1998).

to terms with the source of their false guilt. However, in other cases there is real guilt which has a crippling and imprisoning effect on the individual's life.

Arguably, it is precisely as the awareness of traditional Christian categories of sin, guilt, confession, and forgiveness recede from the popular mindset that the problem of guilt increases. Without the resources of the Christian faith the culture becomes less able to cope with guilt while the problem of guilt feelings becomes more pervasive and harder to deal with. God has been banished from the scene, his remedy for guilt has been discarded, but the guilt does not go away. It remains there stubbornly in the human heart, a disease whose cure has been mislaid.

In my own ministry on a housing estate, a surprising number of people have come to see me to 'confess' their sins. Usually they have not sought formal sacramental confession but their desire to unburden themselves of crippling weights of guilt from the past has been clear. What they have wanted and have needed is forgiveness, the slate wiped clean, a removal of the condemnation they feel and a remedy for their deep feelings of guilt. They want to deal decisively and finally with those things from the past that continue to have such a hold over them in the present. They want it dealt with once and for all.

It is one thing to assure them of God's forgiveness. But how can they be sure? How can they know that their past really has been dealt with? How can they be helped to leave the crippling burden of guilt behind and press on into the future that God has in store for them? It is here that the message of substitution has its particular power and impact.

Guilt and Reparation

People sense that sin must be paid for, that something must be done about it. It is not enough just to say 'forget it,' 'it's in the past,' 'it's over and done with' or even 'God will forgive you.' People instinctively realize that it is not that simple. David Atkinson explains why:

> For guilt to be handled, there must be reparation. The demands of right and wrong must be satisfied. Only then can life go on creatively…. Those strands of the New Testament which speak of the cross in terms of God's curse, of an expression of divine wrath, and of the punishment of sin, are speaking of a divinely provided means by which reparation can be made.[24]

The cross is so satisfying because it speaks to our need for reparation to be made; because it speaks of a cost being paid; because it speaks of sin being *dealt with*, not overlooked or excused, but judged, killed and eradicated.

---

24 Atkinson, D, 'What Difference does the Cross Make to Life?' in Goldingay, J, *op cit*, p 267.

Guilt and a Completed Work

The cross is so satisfying because it speaks of a finished past event. The once-and-for-all-ness of the cross, so emphasized in Hebrews, speaks not only of the cessation of cultic sacrifices but of the finishing and the completion of the work of taking away sin and guilt:

> But now Christ has appeared *once for all* at the end of the ages to do away with sin by the sacrifice of himself.[25]

> We have been made holy through the sacrifice of the body of Jesus *once for all*.[6]

I have often wondered at how Hebrews, which is the most Jewish and in some ways esoteric and even obscure New Testament book, and, therefore, thought by some to be of little contemporary relevance, speaks so powerfully and apparently straightforwardly to the modern heart. Surely it is this emphasis on guilt removed and dealt with finally and decisively—not just merely a ceremonial and outward, cultic, uncleanness but a deep personal and inner guilt—which is so attractive to us and resonates with us to such a large extent.

To our guilt the substitutionary death of Jesus speaks as nothing else can. The power of substitution is that it says *my* sin was dealt with personally by Christ: 'In my place, condemned he stood, sealed my pardon with his blood.'[27] Jesus took *my* sin. Jesus took *my* guilt. Jesus bore the penalty of *my* sin. It has been dealt with decisively there. *My* sin, *my* guilt, *my* judgment is finished with, over and done. I am free, I am forgiven, I am acquitted, and for the man or woman in Christ, there is no more condemnation.[28] This personal identification of the believer with the crucified Lord is, it has already been argued, at the heart of what substitution stands for. And, for the person overwhelmed by guilt, it is the knowledge that their sin and guilt has been carried by Christ on the cross that sets them free.

Substitution and Justice

But is all this just? Critics of penal substitution allege that it fails to abide by even the most elementary rules of justice. It is surely inherently unjust, they argue, for an innocent man to suffer and for the guilty get off scot free. Robert Letham responds:

> ...the guilty do not go free; their guilt is recognized and they are punished with the full sanctions of God's law. The key issue is that they receive this

---

25 Hebrews 9.26.
26 Hebrews 10.10.
27 Bliss, P, *Hymns for Today's Church* (London: Hodder & Stoughton, 1982) No 130.
28 Romans 8.1.

penalty *in Christ*. The fact that he takes the burden of our sins upon himself and undergoes the sanctions God requires should not blind us to the fact that in all he does, it is both as our substitute and our representative. It is the context of a real and vital union between him and us, which is at least as real and vital as that between us and Adam. Hence, we as his people do indeed receive our just deserts for our misdemeanours inasmuch as Christ, having united himself to us in his incarnation, fully discharges the debt we owe.[29]

Karl Barth explains in a similar way how Christ not only takes the place of the guilty sinner and deals with his sinful rebellion once and for all, but how there is a real union between man and Christ to the extent that man can be said to have died *in him:*

> Jesus Christ had taken (man's) place as a malefactor. In his place Jesus Christ has suffered the death of a malefactor. The sentence on him as a sinner has been carried out ... it has fallen ... on Jesus Christ. In and with the man who was taken down dead on Golgotha, man the covenant-breaker is buried and destroyed.[30]

Substitution and Condemnation

Calvin draws attention to a strangely neglected theme—the significance of the *trial* of Christ.[31] First he observes that Christ was manifestly an innocent man. Even Pilate, the man who condemned him, admitted as much:

> Thus we shall behold the person of a sinner and evildoer represented in Christ, yet from his shining innocence it will at the same time be obvious that he was burdened with another man's sin rather than his own.[32]

Next, says Calvin, Christ's condemnation was our condemnation, since he himself was innocent. When he died, he died as our substitute:

> To take away our condemnation, though, it was not enough for him to suffer any kind of death; to make satisfaction for our redemption a form of death had to be chosen in which he might free us both by transferring our condemnation to himself and taking our guilt upon himself.[33]

29 Letham, R, *The Work of Christ* (Leicester: Inter-Varsity Press, 1993) p 136 (my italics).
30 Barth, K (Bromiley, G W and Torrance, T F (eds)), *Church Dogmatics* 1.1 (Edinburgh: T & T Clark, 1956) p 94.
31 Remarkably, few theologians of the atonement have followed Calvin's lead in considering the theological significance of Christ's trial.
32 Calvin, J, *Institutes of the Christian Religion*, Book II (Westminster Press, 1960) 16.5.
33 Calvin, *op cit*, 16.5.

Some theologians have criticized an over-emphasis on legal categories in thinking about the atonement.[34] Calvin makes the point that the passion included a real legal event—a trial. Legal categories were there at the heart of the event—they have not been artificially imported from outside. It may be that Calvin's understanding of the significance of Christ's trial will resonate strongly with those who, like Christ, have been condemned unjustly through a corrupt legal process. They know what it is to be declared guilty, though they are innocent. In the cross, they can find what it is to be declared innocent, though guilty, through what Jesus went through in their place.

Whatever may be the cause of our guilt, the good news of substitution is that the work of dealing with it is completed and finished. Calvin emphasizes the pastoral significance of substitution in the reassurance it brings to the troubled soul:

> This is our acquittal; the guilt that held us liable for punishment has been transferred to the head of the Son of God. We must, above all, remember this substitution, lest we tremble and remain anxious throughout life—as if God's righteous vengeance, which the Son of God has taken upon himself, still hung over us.[35]

Substitution and the Past

One criticism offered of a penal substitutionary understanding of the atonement is that it is essentially 'backward rather than forward looking.'[36] It speaks of the dealing with sins in the past but appears in itself to say nothing about the personal transformation of the life of the believer in the future. One answer to that objection is to say that penal substitution is not to be taught in isolation; other aspects of the biblical revelation that concern sanctification and spiritual growth must be taught *as well* if the whole counsel of God is to be proclaimed. But another answer is to say that the backward looking orientation of the substitutionary atonement is in fact its greatest strength.

In dealing with guilt, so often we are working with the effects of past events. Substitution addresses these by proclaiming the effect of the past and finished event of the cross. Precisely, because what Christ did is a finished event *in the past*, believers who see themselves united to Christ in his death can look at the cross and see their own Saviour substituting himself there. Such persons can have real confidence that the events of the past that have such a hold over them in terms of guilt are finished and dealt with. They died with Christ on the cross. Their power to hurt and wound, to burden with guilt and shame, has been broken.

---

34 See for example Smail, T, 'Can One Man Die for the People ?' in Goldingay, J, *op cit.*
35 Calvin, *op cit*, 16.5.
36 Smail, T, *op cit*, p 95.

In fact, it is our past—our constant looking back to what has happened *then*—that most prevents our enjoyment of life *now*. But a backward look to the cross, where the believer's past was dealt with decisively by Christ, enables him or her not only to face the future but to go confidently into it and say, with St Paul: 'Forgetting what is behind and straining towards what is ahead; I press on towards the goal.'[37] This is possible because the past is dealt with.

This is not to say, of course, that the past has no continuing effect on the believer from thereon. We are all affected by our past in so many ways. The past can leave an indelible mark on our character or effect a permanent change in our circumstances or relationships. God freely grants forgiveness for our sins but, in this life, we often have no choice but to live with the consequences of both our own sin and that of others. However, the believer who has brought his or her past to the foot of the cross can be free of the *guilt* associated with those past events. This in itself gives a new perspective on the past and frees the individual to go forward into the future with hope.

As one young man in our church who had been a Christian for just a few days, and who had been seriously troubled by his past, told me:

> You can put your old self back in the past. That was then, this is now. You can get on with your life. All the bad things are put to death on the cross but all the good things come from the cross like joy and forgiveness.[38]

All this accords with the Pauline understanding of the Lord's supper as the proclamation of a past event with a future orientation: 'whenever you eat this bread and drink this cup you proclaim the Lord's death until he comes.'[39] The past event is proclaimed whenever believers meet to share in the supper. Their fresh knowledge of the death of Christ and what it means and what it has achieved for them is meat and drink for them in their journey through life into God's future, *when he comes* (and to the final and complete outworking of God's plan of redemption at the end of the age). Renewal of life and faith comes to believers who look back and remember what God has done for them.

Substitution and New Life

Ultimately the message of the cross is a message of sins forgiven, of condemnation lifted and of a new life to be lived. The particular value of substitution is that it enables us to assure individuals that their sins have been dealt with personally, decisively and completely. It is the basis for their assurance. It is no wonder that the sense of assurance, such a hallmark of evangelical religion, is so clearly linked with the preaching of substitution.

---

37 Philippians 3.13.
38 Personal interview.
39 1 Corinthians 11.26.

No one has better described the power of the cross in the life of the believer, the joy of sins forgiven and of a burden lifted, than John Bunyan:

…just as Christian came up with the cross, his burden loosed from his shoulders and fell from his back… Then was Christian glad and lightsome, and said with a merry heart 'He hath given me rest, by his sorrow, and life, by his death.' Then he stood still for a while to look and wonder; for it was very surprising to him that the sight of the Cross should thus ease his burden. He looked, therefore, and looked again, even till the springs that were in his head sent the water down his cheeks. Now as he stood looking and weeping, behold three Shining Ones came to him and saluted him with 'Peace be to thee.' So the first said to him 'Thy sins be forgiven.' The second stripped him of his rags and gave him a change of raiment… Then Christian gave three leaps for joy and went on singing:

> *Thus far did I come loaden with my sin*
> *Nor could aught else ease the grief that I was in,*
> *Till I come hither. What a place is this!*
> *Must here be the beginning of my bliss?*
> *Must here the burden fall from off my back?*
> *Must here the strings that bound it to me, crack?*
> *Blessed Cross! Blessed Sepulchre! Blessed rather be*
> *The man that there was put to shame for me.*[40]

Mark's Story

But now to a contemporary witness from my own church. Mark said, 'I felt I had done a lot of bad things in my life and all of a sudden there was an opportunity for me to have a new start because of what this guy had done on the cross. Before I became a Christian I could picture the things I had done in the past, people I had hurt, the guilt was just holding on to me. The guilt used to play over and over in my head. I remember something I did as a teenager coming back from a football match. I threw a rock which hit a woman. At the time it seemed a good laugh but later I carried the guilt for years.'

'The amazing thing about the cross was that the end of someone else started a new beginning for me. It's knowing your sins are paid for, having assurance. It's freedom—from the guilt . The guilt used to play over and over in my head but now I know I can come to the cross and confess it and Jesus will take it on himself. When I think of the cross I think of the pain he was prepared to endure for me. He did it 2000 years ago but he has done it for us now.'[41]

---

40 Bunyan, John, *Pilgrim's Progress* (London: Penguin, 1965, (first published 1678)) p 82.
41 Personal interview.

4

Substitution and True Worth

A tragic effect of the large-scale break up of family relationships in urban communities is the growing number of broken, hurt and battered people.

Clergy and other professionals who work in urban areas are only too aware of this. On the estate where I live primary school headteachers tell me that they spend significant amounts of their time counselling parents about difficult relationships at home. These relationships often break up in great acrimony and cause terrible hurt to both the participants and their children and step-children. This produces more and more deeply disturbed children in schools at a younger and younger age. In due course, these children grow up to be parents themselves and so the cycle of insecurity and instability continues.

If present trends continue, there are likely to be even more damaged and broken people in the future who will have suffered from a lack of love, the abuse of love or the fracture of love. Such people frequently struggle with deep feelings of low self-worth or even self-loathing and hatred.

'You're nothing'

Members of my congregation have told me how throughout childhood and into adult life they had been told repeatedly, 'you're no good, you're useless, you're nothing.' This message has been given explicitly and verbally over and over again by close members of their own family until they have come to believe it. Countless others have received the same message—more subtly, but no less damagingly—through their experience of education, work, family life, and even, most tragically of all, the church. They have come to the same conclusion.

Others have been the victims of degrading sexual practices which have left them feeling dirty and shamed. A forty-year-old woman in the parish told me recently how a lifetime of childhood sexual abuse and adult physical abuse and mental cruelty had left her, in her words, with 'no self-worth at all.'

For others, it is the sheer impersonality of modern life, the experience of being a very small cog in a vast machine, that has left them feeling small, marginalized, of little significance or account. The many dehumanizing effects of modern society add to this: the replacement of human contact by computer technology, the replacement of the corner shop by the out of town mega-store, the remote Council bureaucracy that runs the estate, the decline of community organizations and the increasing atomization of society.

For still others, it is the sense of personal failure that leaves them defeated. Failure at school, failure in the workplace, failure in marriage, failure as a parent—all these experiences can rob someone of any real sense of self-worth or personal significance.

And with all this there can be deep failings of shame :

> Shame ... expresses the division between my hopes, desires, aspirations and my failures, falling short and disappointment. Shames makes it hard for me to sing 'Thank you, Father, for making me me.' Through my own wrong doing as well as my failure to achieve, I believe myself to be of little worth.[42]

Many people in urban priority areas (and elsewhere) feel this way. To them the message of the substitutionary death of Christ speaks directly with power because it speaks of their true worth in the sight of God.

'You're special'

Graham Kendrick's song for children, *I'm special,* captures something of the power of substitution in the lives of those who feel worthless and lacking in significance:

> *I'm special because God has loved me*
> *For he gave the best thing that he had to save me;*
> *His own Son, Jesus, crucified to take the blame*
> *For all the bad things I have done*
>
> *Thank you Jesus, thank you Lord*
> *For loving me so much*
> *I know I don't deserve anything.*
> *Help me feel your love right now,*
> *To know deep in my heart*
> *That I'm your special friend.*[43]

My dream as the pastor of an urban church is for every member of our congregation to be able to sing that song from their hearts and know it to be true, for them, *because of Jesus.* David Atkinson comments:

> If sin is about shame, forgiveness ... is about the development of a realistic self concept. It is about knowing myself as united with the crucified and risen Lord, with my identity now given, not through my own division and failure, but in grace.[44]

Christina Baxter, speaking about women's experience of salvation, describes how the message of the cross brings an understanding of true worth and value:

---

42 Atkinson, *op cit,* p 263.
43 Kendrick, G, *Songs of Fellowship* (Eastbourne: Kingsway Music, 1998) No 236.
44 Atkinson, *op cit,* p 264.

…the model of redemption brings to me the knowledge that I am bought with a price which gives me a sense of worth and value which diminishes the praise of those around me and draws the sting of their condemnation. Redeemed by God … women are enabled to have a sense of worth which is not always given to them by the society in which they live.[45]

A Personal Message

Most theories of atonement see the cross as an expression of divine love. As has already been argued, the distinctiveness of a substitutionary understanding of the atonement is that it explains precisely *how* the cross is such an expression and does so in directly personal and relational terms. It is not simply that the cross is an expression of heroic self-sacrifice whereby Jesus expressed, in some rather vague and unformed way, a general love for humanity in general. Still less is it merely an outstanding act of love for us to admire and emulate (a merely exemplarist doctrine of the atonement is surely cold comfort to those who feel unloved or guilty or unable to love). Rather it is that wonderful news that 'the son of God loved me and gave himself for *me*.'[46]

It was for *me* that Jesus died. He died in *my* place and in so doing he showed not only how much he loved me but also how much I was truly worth. This is of profound pastoral significance in ministering to those who believe themselves to be worth nothing. To be able to say 'this is how much Jesus thought you were worth. He was willing to die for you. He gave that much. That was his estimation of your true worth. If your experience of life so far tells you that you are worthless, the cross tells you how much you are really worth to God.' In the words of another Kendrick song: 'he paid what he thought you were worth.'[47]

Where people, for all sorts of reasons, have not experienced love and find themselves unloved, the message of substitution is that God loved them personally and showed it:

God has *shown* us how much he loves—it was while we were still sinners that Christ died for us![48]

To come to the cross and to see it in a substitutionary way is to experience the fullness of God's love and to know our true worth before him.

The Cross and Communion

Traditionally, the eucharist or Lord's supper has been understood as the sacrament of the atonement. Frequently, though not always, this has been

45 Baxter, C, 'Jesus the Man and Women's Salvation,' in Goldingay, J, *op cit*, p 145.
46 Galatians 2.20.
47 Kendrick, G, 'How much do you think you are worth?' in *Paid on the nail* (Audio cassette) (Eastbourne: Kingsway, 1974).
48 Romans 5.8 (*Good News Bible*).

understood in specifically substitutionary terms.[49] Some Christian traditions have increasingly downplayed this focus on the atonement (whilst not denying it altogether) in favour of greater concentration on the incarnation. Here the communion is seen as, above all, the sacrament of the *presence* of the Lord.[50] However, this trend presents a real danger, namely the risk of diminishing the effectiveness of the sacrament of the Lord's supper as a reminder and pledge of the love of God at the very time that we need it most.

The 1662 *Prayer Book* liturgy of the Church of England speaks of the elements of bread and wine as 'pledges of his love' which are given 'for a continual remembrance of his death to our great and endless comfort.'[51] Rightly understood and properly celebrated the Lord's supper, as a proclamation of the Lord's death, is a powerful means of conveying the full pastoral impact of substitution. The essential message conveyed by the elements at holy communion is 'Jesus loved you enough to die for you.' Any diminution of the cross-centredness of eucharistic liturgies will tend to reduce their effectiveness in conveying this vital message.

True Worth

The Church of England Doctrine Commission's report *The Mystery of Salvation* described the worth accorded to us by God in the act of redemption thus :

> Not only does he make explicit the worth he has already assigned to us in creating us, he declares that worth to be absolute in his eyes despite all the evidence we have created to the contrary. There we are freed for a new future, one in which we can now be confident of our own worth, that value has been accorded us by God, and so there ceases to be any need for self-justification, for in any sense proving to others or to God that we are indeed of some importance.[52]

What the Cross Means to Me

I leave the last word in this section to a member of my church, Leslie, who explains what the substitutionary death of Jesus means to him: 'It shows us how much God loves us. As a father myself, I think how much it must have cost God

---

49 See for example the appendix 'Salvation and the Anglican Heritage' in the Church of England's Doctrine Commission report, *The Mystery of Salvation* (London: Church House Publishing, 1995) which discusses the use of substitutionary and penal ideas in the Articles of Religion and the prayer books of 1549, 1552, and 1662.

50 Traditional Catholicism has had a particular emphasis on the incarnation and on the presence of Christ in the Holy Communion, witness the Roman doctrine of transubstantiation, for example, but this has often been coupled with a robust doctrine of atonement, as well. It is in the more liberal forms of Catholicism, especially in Anglicanism, that atonement theology has been sharply downgraded in favour of incarnation and presence.

51 From the exhortation at Holy Communion in the *Book of Common Prayer*, 1662.

52 Doctrine Commission of the General Synod of the Church of England, *op cit*, p 124.

to allow Jesus to die on the cross. God's love for us is more than we can imagine. Jesus knew what he was doing when he went to the cross and to do that for us is the ultimate love. You sometimes hear of someone putting themselves into someone else's place but Jesus did that for all of us.

'It gives me peace and security. It's a security that cannot be broken. You know you belong. You know you're loved. You know you have eternal life now. Someone has given their life for you. He didn't have to do it but he did because he loved us. I think how much he loved us to be willing to die in that way.'[53]

---

53 Personal interview.

5
Substitution and the Praise-Filled Life

Jesus, what can I give, what can I bring
To so faithful a friend, to so loving a king?
Saviour, what can be said, what can be sung
as a praise of your name
For the things you have done
Oh, my words could not tell, not even in part
Of the debt of love that is owed by this thankful heart.

You deserve my every breath
For you've paid the great cost;
Giving up your life to death
even death on the cross.[54]

The spirituality of substitution is one of deep praise and thanksgiving to God. It is a spirituality of personal indebtedness to Christ. It is a spirituality that inspires sacrificial living and giving. It is a spirituality that leads, in short, to worship. George Carey explains:

> …the love of a representative is generous enough but the love of a substitute, who takes my sin and makes it his and who becomes 'God forsaken' is beyond the realm of human language, but thankfully not worship.[55]

The spirituality of substitution inspires the believer to a sacrificial offering of himself to God in thanksgiving for his indescribable gift. In *Pilgrim's Progress* Hopeful's sense of gratitude to the substitute who 'died the death … not for himself but for me'[56] issues in a desire to glorify Christ and live a holy life:

> And now was my heart full of joy, mine eyes full of tears, and my affections running over with love, to the name, people and ways of Jesus Christ…. It made me love a holy life, and long to do something for the honour and glory of the name of the Lord Jesus.[57]

---

54 Redman, M, 'I will offer up my life,' *Songs of Fellowship*, No 851.
55 Carey, G, *The Gate of Glory* (London: Hodder & Stoughton, 1986) p 154.
56 Bunyan, *op cit*, p 192.
57 Bunyan, *op cit*, p 195.

James Packer notes:

> The notion which the phrase penal substitution expresses is that Jesus Christ our Lord, moved by a love that was determined to do everything necessary to save us, endured and exhausted the destructive divine judgment, for which we were otherwise inescapably destined, and so won us forgiveness, adoption, and glory. To affirm penal substitution is to say that believers are in debt to Christ specifically for this and that this is the mainspring of all their joy, peace, and praise both now and for eternity.[58]

The power of the spirituality of substitution to inspire the believer to sacrificial acts of service to God and the community, to generous financial giving, and even to the laying down of life in perilous missionary circumstances is well known. Michael Saward argues that there is a direct correlation between the level of giving and the preaching of a message of redemption centred on the cross:

> For many years the stewardship movement has laid great stress on the goodness of God in creation. It has not ... made much of the redemptive act of God in Christ. I am personally convinced that the one thing that has always been the deepest motivational challenge to Christians has been the redeeming work of Christ's *death* and the power of his subsequent resurrection....
>
> Jesus paid a price beyond all reckoning and we in gratitude give ourselves as a thank-offering. Moved by that conviction Christians have gone to the ends of the earth. It is the supreme motivation of Christian living and giving.[59]

The spirituality of substitution springs from a deep knowledge and awareness of God's love which itself evokes a response of love. This surely is true worship. This is the basis of St Paul's exhortation in Romans 12. In the first eleven chapters of the letter he describes the grace and mercy of God shown in Christ, then in chapter 12 he exhorts his readers to respond in the only appropriate way:

> Therefore, I urge you, brothers, *in view of God's mercy*, to offer your bodies as living sacrifices, holy and pleasing to God—this is your spiritual act of worship.[60]

58 Packer, *op cit*, p 25.
59 Saward, M, *All Change: The Local Church Changes Gear* (London: Hodder & Stoughton, 1983) p 75.
60 Romans 12.1.

And so the spirituality of substitution leads the believer to sing:

Were the whole realm of nature mine,
That were an offering far too small;
Love so amazing, so divine,
Demands my soul, my life, my all.[61]

61 Watts, I, *Hymns for Today's Church* (London: Hodder & Stoughton, 1982) No 147.